THE UBER DIARIES
ATLANTA EDITION

NICO TAYLOR

Taylor Made Publishing LLC

LITHONIA GA

To the Roots in my life. My wife Renisha I love you more each day. My Queen, Mi Amor.

My Queen Mother Mary Emma. You have played every part in my orchestra of life. Thank you for opening the gates of knowledge unto me. For you I am eternally grateful.

Nico

Rest in Paradise Mama
MARY E. TAYLOR
Sunrise August 29, 1940 - Sunset April 14, 2019

CONTENTS

INTRODUCTION

In today's world balancing your professional life and your social life is harder than ever. Not to mention Atlanta traffic, rush hour(s), accidents, school busses, kids, lunch time rush, non-At-Alien implants (that never seem to get use to the flow of city traffic!), just plain awful drivers. Last but certainly not least that congested construction traffic that happens to be on every other exit to YOUR destination! Lucky us!

Nowadays, all these factors are constant in the "A", as well as many other growing metropolitan areas in the world. Right up there in the forefront of my necessities in life. You know? Water, air, food, love, sex, family and UBER.

I mean really, in the past 3 years, when was the last time you have been driving down the street and you DIDN'T see a car with an UBER decal in the window?? I'll answer that question for you.

NEVER!!

Needless to say, a bit more sporadic; however inevitable you'll see the other rideshare decals in the streets of Atlanta as well. From Lyft, to Juno to Zimride and those little fast ass annoying scooters!

From a rideshare driver perspective the experience is extremely unique. So unique that you never know what or who you're going to get. After performing my 1000th rideshare trip I noticed something.... My roles changed pretty much ride by ride.!

What do I mean by that? Over the past two years and 1200 different rideshare experiences I have had to be a chameleon and wear many colors. For instance, I have been a counselor, a therapist, a friend, life coach, mother figure, the cool chic with good music, an alibi, a news reporter, a bouncer, ambulance/medic, rescue, and sometimes just the voice of reason on a wild Friday night.

Whatever the fare, thankfully I've been up for the challenge. Being a veteran driver in Atlanta, there is no shortage of amazing things I've encountered over the years. Here are a few of my wildest encounters that were memorable for one reason or another.

WARNING

You are about to read a book that is funny as hell. All of the stories in this book are true and actual encounters. I was an Uber driver between the years 2014-2017. In no way am I condoning or promoting my behavior as a driver to other drivers. My actions are my own.

The stops are documented with detail according to my recollection and notes of the encounter. The names of the riders have been altered to protect their identities and my ass.

ENJOY!

CHAPTER ONE

A BEAUTIFUL DAY TO GO AWOL

Pickup Location: 232 Forsyth Street
Greyhound Station
Time: 11:48 PM

Today has been a beautiful day in Atlanta. Sunny all day and by now nightfall has proved to be equally as beautiful as the day. Temperatures still clocking in at about 78 degrees and its almost midnight.

Only in Hotlanta baby.

God, I love this city. Definitely my second home.

Rideshare driving fulltime, 5-6 days a week can have its ups and downs. Especially if you're anything like me and have never driven a car for a living.

Don't get me wrong, I'm pretty well versed professionally. I have managed fortune 500companies in the restaurant, retail, home improvement, gas and diesel fuel travel plazas. Heavy equipment rental, dry cleaning, HVAC sales both residential and commercial. As well as consulting business owners and managers to streamline their business practices.

Still nothing like driving Uber.

Every other professional position I have ever been in has been pretty consistent day in day out duties. To me, that's what the definition of work is, Tasks!!

Not Uber.

Unpredictable Always.

This particular day started early for me. My wife and I went to the city to hangout. Work hard play hard is one of the mottos for my life. I wanna live young, wild and free.

Everything's poppin downtown. So many people out walking down here. I'm sure all the extra commotion and crowded streets are due to the "Home Team". There was a game earlier at the Dome and the Falcons won! (The Dome is what the stadium was called before the remodel.)

Our new sports arena; The Falcons Mercedes Benz Stadium. The remodeled venue is even bigger and more beautiful than before and we have a retractable rooftop on this thing! The Mercedes Benz Stadium is truly a sight to see.

The city is always lit when we win a game. This year the Falcons are really bringing the noise. Two words. Devonte Freeman. 'Nuff said.

For real, the city is on fire! Light's everywhere! Time to yell ACTION!

I lived on the south side at this time. So usually I would start my trips at the airport or something like that. Tonight, was different though.

When I got on the road to drive for the night it was about 8:30pm. Everything about tonight feels different and is different, so I decided to take a different approach. Decision made, I will not to go to the airport tonight, I'm just gonna ride a little further and get off at Turner Field. I'm hoping to catch some bar hoppers celebrating the big win!

After giving the car a quick onceover and restocking my H2O, I hit the For-Hire button on my app.

My first pickup was two college kids going downtown to pick up some food from a local pizzeria. Brad and Corey were the rider's names and they both attend Georgia Tech. They are frat brothers.

The house where I picked them up was every bit of what it appeared to be. There were beer cans thrown out on the front lawn and what appeared to be toilet paper rolled in the trees and hedges that surround the entry to the front doorway.

That couldn't be a frat house. Could it?

The ride is a total of about 11 minutes. Pickup and drop off, together. We really didn't have much time to mingle.

The same frat house I picked the duo up is there drop off location as well.

When we pulled into the driveway at the frat house, the beer bottles say this party has already been underway a while, and it's time for intermission. So now, this group is complete.

The guys had a nice group waiting outside to intercept the 6 pizzas. All Corey and Brad could do was shake their heads and laugh as they close the car door.

All that effort and you still might have to fight for a piece of the pie! Lesson learned for me was if you have greedy friends, always order a separate meal. It doesn't pay to be a hungry errand boy.

Night fellas be safe.

On to the next.

I decided to turn around and head towards Mechanicsville. I'm back online, and as soon as I hit the For-Hire button (and spray a little Lysol to get that funky pizza smell outta my ride) I get another request. I accept.

The pickup location is familiar for a few reasons. One very fundamental fact being that it's the address to the ONLY Greyhound station in Atlanta. Forsyth Street.

Very memorable location. Shit, just Forsyth Street in general is memorable.

There are about 4-5 other streets in Atlanta with similar reputations. You know, those one liner streets that people say to make your eyes light up and shit. Dirty words like Metropolitan, Edgewood, Bankhead FIB (Fulton Industrial Blvd) and Memorial Dr.

Anybody who's even a lil' familiar looks at you like whoa, I wouldn't be caught DEAD over there after dark!

The bus station itself seems like a hangout, or a little micro sized airport. It seriously does when you sit back and look at it. This place is always busy!

From the characters you see outside the bus station, just hanging out. To the equally high traffic building directly across the street...

The forever infamous strip club, "Magic City".

Boy, I tell you. I have had some epic moments in that building on a Monday. Forget about it!!

I digress ......

CMMM HMMM. As I clear my throat, back to business.

The riders name is Ryan. There are no parking spots free in the lot by the station. I'm familiar with the area so I parked on the side street directly across from the parking lot. On Garnett Street where I'm parked, I can see everything at the station.

Ryan called me only a few moments after I got comfy on Garnett. He was direct and to the point. Only saying, "I'm coming out of the restroom and headed straight for the front door. I have on a blue baseball cap and a large green duffle bag."

I said ok and asked Ryan to stay on the phone until he saw my car.

After hearing his description, I was immediately able to notice Ryan through the crowd.

"I can see you clearly Ryan. If you look directly across the street, I'm sitting in the grey four door Malibu. I just threw my hazards on. Can you see me?"

Ryan said, "Yup, I'm walking over."

I opened the trunk for the rider's bag and offered Ryan a drink as he got in and closed the passenger side door.

Alright. So where are we headed??

He reaches in his top right pocket and pulls out a piece of crumbled up paper.

"Hold on, I'm putting the address in now."

Okay got it!"

The app chimes with a new destination.

Alrighty Ryan, thanks for the update. Buckle up my friend. We have quite a ride. About 55 min till we arrive.

He seemed to be a talker right off the bat. He told me that the address we are in route to is his besties place. He said they have been friends since birth and this guy knows everything about him.

Then Ryan started filling me in on his best friend, Ben, in detail. He says, "my best friend just moved, this will be my first time at his new place. His girlfriend dumped him, so he had to move quickly. He says this place is a dump, but I guess we'll see when we get there."

Okay, cool I thought with a little chuckle.

Where are you traveling from Ryan?

Langley, he said quickly and reversed the curse by saying D.C. area. As if to say, you're a civilian. You wouldn't know the reference to Langley.

Little does Ryan know I have a military family. I never enlisted myself, although I was an extremely promising solider in my high school ROTC class.

The thought of getting up for rollcall and PT has never been my bag. Besides, I've always prided myself on being an individual. I write the vision. I set the objective for my personal development, and I don't like to stand stagnant, or where directed.

As Ryan, made his way out of the bus station I noticed that the duffle he was carrying was military issued. Green and huge. There is no mistaking an army duffle.

My next response was, Oh, so you're on leave, eh? How long?

Ryan said slowly, "Not…. Exactly… On leave." He said it so peculiar that I had to say "Huh?", as if I didn't hear him just to get the confirmation I was looking for.

Sure enough our Billy boy said not exactly, but only this time he added," It was more like I just left!"

WOW!!

Just left huh? That's called AWOL, I'm pretty sure that's frowned upon.

One of my uncles went AWOL and as a kid I remember MP's that weren't very friendly coming and hauling his naked ass from the basement in the middle of the night! Not a very pretty scene when your 4 yrs. old.

The memory of being awakened by loud pounding on the front door is literally unforgettable.

It was wintertime, during Christmas break. I was staying over my grandmas for the holiday weekend. At the time I didn't have my own room at my grandmas, so I slept in the bed with her. Naturally with all the commotion when she jumped up, it awakened me too. Always being sure to stay just a few steps behind my granny I followed her downstairs to see what was going on.

The pounding on the front door came from two males in hats with rifles and white letters on their sleeves that read MP. Their facial expressions confirmed there were zero games being played.

There was one white officer and one black officer. They asked my grandma a total of two or three questions at the door.

The first question was is this person here? The white MP pulled out a photograph of my uncle from his top jacket pocket to confirm. The second question was are you his mother?

Quickly my grandmother confessed "YES" to both questions! As a child I don't remember thinking twice about her answers. In my current state of mind, I'm like damn grandma you didn't even hesitate to give up your own son!

It's a hard knock life!

Now that I think back the third question they asked was if they could enter.

Again, she said YES.

The officers rushed into our home and performed a search and seizure like some cat and mouse shit. One at a time. In every, single, room of the house. Peek-A-Boo!

I remember the encounter being extremely brief. They had one objective and they reached it quickly. They found the perp! My uncle. Ironically this negro was hiding under the bed! Even back then he wasn't very clever.

The last scene was my uncle; handcuffed with no shirt being escorted to the military truck out front in 30-degree New York winter weather.

Quite the White Christmas.

To this day my vivid memories of seeing my uncle; drenched with sweat, black socks, white boxers and seeming in a panic as he struggled in handcuffs with two men assisting him thru the front door is still a daunting memory.

Back then my thoughts were different. Today I have only one word; CONTROL.

It's so funny how we can recall some events for a lifetime, and others fade away in moments.

Ryan said my story made him realize that so many people are negatively affected by things. Things they never liked or agreed to. Things they can't forget. Things that they just grow to adapt to. Things they never can remember to change.

Then Ryan sits back and says, "But as for me, I just had to go. That place isn't right. They tried to fuck with my mind. Brainwash me. They give me all these tests to see if was "compatible" with the programming. The more you resist, the more of a test dummy you become".

I personally can't stand for someone to try and play mind games with me. If you wanna play games like that, count me out.

My actual response was "Damn for real, Ryan? Man, I'm telling you that sounds crazy bro."

Ryan said, "I had to get the fuck outta there. I don't give a damn how many simulations we go thru. I'm never gonna say or think killing a kid is an acceptable practice."

"No, not me. I'm not a good fit. I'll never be a good fit."

Brother, I must tell you, from the sound of that. I am not a good fit either.

Less than 3 minutes left in the ride and I only have one question burning in my mind for Ryan. So, I asked; How did you get away and what are you gonna do now, Ryan?

He said, "I'm gonna stay under ground and tunnel like they taught me. Get lost, stay free."

GPS sounds off again. "Destination is on your right."

Ryan says nothing, he just reaches his hand over the back of my seat and pulls me in for a hug.

"Thanks Nico take care."

Just like a sound or a flash of light my door closed, and Ryan disappeared into the night's darkness. I pray the darkness covers you brother stay safe, be well.

PRO DRIVER TIP 1

As a driver, it is so important to be in "the KNOW".
So, keep yourself abreast of all current events in your city.
It's smart to go where the $Money is.

CHAPTER TWO

MOM!! WTF!?!

Pickup Location: Stagecoach
Buckhead, Atlanta
Time: 2:15 AM

Ahh, yes!!! Buckhead traffic at 2am. This is the life!

I've been out all night and now is crunch time! Early morning club rush.

This ride started off typical. Pickup 2 males and a female. The contact name is Jake. I got the request after a short ride from Vining's to Mt. Paran.

Man…. You can hardly drive thru Buckhead sometimes, because drunk people are walking in the streets!

There are a lot of people out here tonight. I better park and call the rider, make it easy on myself.

I pull into Henry's (Haan-rees) Bakery parking lot just ahead and park to call the rider.

Ring, ring." Hello, this is Nico your Uber driver. Is this Jake?"

"Yes, this is Jake the guy replies, we're coming out now".

OK cool, I'm in a silver Chevy, black tint. I'll have the hazards on for you. Parked in front on Henry's Bakery right across the street from where you are.

"Ok thanks" Jake replied.

Moments later three people are approaching my vehicle and a fairly handsome gentlemen, 6 feet with long locs and hazel eyes opens the passenger side door and says: "What's up? I'm Jake, we're going to be splitting the fare, and we will need to make two stops, if that's cool?

Com'on in guys no worries. Put the first stop in the app, and when we arrive you will need to change the destination.

"Ok, thanks Nico."

Everybody buckles up for safety.

First stop is about a good 30minute ride from here. Music playing low in the background, the wind whipping through the back of the car with the windows down. Other than that, the backseat was so quiet you could literally hear a mouse pissing on cotton! Absolutely NO conversation.

When I looked in my rear view all I could see was cell phone lights and Jake grinding his teeth and breathing deeply. The female sits in between the two fellas in the back seat. Tension is thick, I mean REAL thick. The kind you can cut with a knife, you know that kind.... QUIET.

Then all of a sudden, BOOP! Sounded like someone just got punched in the face.

YOOOO!!! I quickly replied. Do we need to pull the hell over?

Not a sound from anyone and I'm not sure what all this anger is about but my intuition tells me to keep quiet and ask later if the opportunity arises. For now, keep with the atmosphere.

"You have arrived at your destination", the GPS sounds.

The driver side rear door swings open. Male exits quietly holding his face, without a word being said. I was thinking as he exited, "You're gonna just let him do you like that dude?

Jake and the female remained in the car.

Sooo, Jake? Have you changed that destination yet buddy? I didn't hear the update in the app.

"Sorry" Nico, Jake replied.

"I'm so fucking mad I can't see straight! I got you though, we're all set now".

Uber app sounds for an added route. GPS sounds again

"We're all set, drive safely.", and we're on the road again...

Jake is a lot more sociable this time around. He starts to tell me why he is so upset with the guy we just dropped off.

Jake screams out,

"Fuck!! I should've punched that mother fucker in the mouth again!"

The female begins to console Jake in the back seat. Her name is Jess, and she says to Jake "Baby, you did good. If you would've hit him again, you would be in trouble now and not riding home in an Uber". (Women are so insightful, no wonder we are the givers of life. Most of us have an intuition when it comes to diffusing a situation).

Naturally. Wow was my response. What did that guy do? I want to make sure I don't do it!

Jake responds with.

"That piece of shit use to be my best friend, before I moved to Costa Rica for two years. I left to fulfill my dreams as a photographer. After two and a half years I returned back to Atlanta yesterday to find out that my childhood best friend and my MOM are in a relationship!!"

"What the FUCK!!"

"I want to bash his fucking face in!!".

"He told me yesterday he had something to tell me and asked if I wanted to meet at Stagecoach our old hangout spot. I said sure, I mean this guy was my roommate, best friend, confidant, my bro."

"I sublet my room in the apartment we shared, so this fucker didn't have to worry about my half of the rent."

"I didn't get at his sister when she basically stalked me for 3 years. That's what bros are supposed to do. We look out for each other."

"We DON'T fuck each other's MOMS!"

"I mean I can't believe this jerk. All the woman in Atlanta. Shit ALL the women in the world, and he chooses my mom?"

How crazy is that shit??

An asshole like me, just sits there at the red light with my mouth hanging open. Like what do you say in response to that? Talk about the ultimate disrespect and disloyalty to your best friend.

Meanwhile I'm thinking....

Best friends?! Then you sleep with the woman that baked you, and the homie cookies! Took you home from football practice and sent you home before curfew?

How does that work??

What does that make you, getting serious with my mom?

My stepdaddy??

OVER MY DEAD BODY!!

A 23-yr. old guy and you choose a 55+ yr. old woman.? Have you seen all this young ass in the "A"? I mean seriously, A real Mrs. Robinson.

Some shit is just stranger than fiction.

GPS sounds again, "In 1000ft your destination is on the right"

Listen Jake, you seem like a good guy. Don't let other people's actions force you into making irrational decisions. You have so much to gain from this beautiful love by your side that you met on your journey in Costa Rica. Build off that Jake.

Good luck to the both of you.

"Thanks Nico, you're awesome".

Take care you guys!

Doors close and I end the ride in the Uber app.

MOM WTF!!

PRO DRIVER TIP 2

It's okay to ask for a Five Star Rating!
It's kind of like asking for the sale.
And you GOTTA ask for the sale!

If there is no reason the rider shouldn't rate you
high, what's the harm in asking??

CHAPTER THREE

HIT AND RUN

Pick Up Location: Marta Station, Georgia Tech.
Time: 9:22 PM

The night seems still in Atlanta.

It's a Hump Day and I'm starting my night at the airport. The streets are so quiet, it seems like the city is headed to bed early.

Clear streets. The air is still, and the sky is dusk.

Coming back to the dorm from a peaceful winter break at home with mom and dad. That was the story for my quiet first ride. The trip ended at Georgia Tech. A young freshman college kid. Only sentiment was" back to reality kid".

What I actually said was," Be safe and good luck with your studies Dylan".

Beep, Beep, Beep, Beep. There goes $$. Second pickup was the Marta (Metropolitan Atlanta Rail and Transit Authority) Station about 3 minutes away. The call was immediate, so it seems like the area is rocking right now. Even though I don't see anyone on the streets. I'll' take the bait.

If I can have a steady flow of riders tonight, no matter if their short trips. It'll still be worth my time tonight. Gotta get some points on the score board.

I'm set from earlier. I've got my h2o, mints and I have subscribed to Pandora. So, the tunes are endless, and they play a nice little variety. Easy listening solution. Just so you don't get bored with the monotony of the whole thing. With Pandora I just pick my genre or artist and I am jamming until I say STOP!

I picked some ol' skool R&B tonight. I'm moving to Jagged Edge and Dru Hill. Always loved Dru Hill. (You know that quiet pause as one of your all-time favorite songs begin to play) ... Oh shit, my song! Beauty's gone.... I wish I never told you, you should leave, I wish you never.... You know the lyrics, definitely a fav. Saved!!

Pulling up now and calling the rider. Hey this is Nico, your Uber driver.

Is this Melissa?

"Yes, this is Melissa. I am out front on the Peachtree Street side.".

I'm on Peachtree too Melissa.

I'm driving a silver Chevy. I parked at the bottom of the stairs and I just put the hazards on.

"I see you Nico, I'm on the stairs walking down towards you".

I see you too. Awesome!

Melissa opens the door and hops right in.

As I greeted Melissa with a hey there! I went ahead and pressed the green start mark and started the ride. Is this the correct destination Melissa? I asked before I pulled into traffic.

"Yes ma'am". Melissa replied. "I'm headed home to Alpharetta."

Ok cool.

I turned my blinker on and headed in the opposite direction, towards the "Varsity". I'll be able to catch I-85 and head towards 400N. It can be a zoo around this time. I tend to think everyone's headed home from a night on the town. You know, eating at some fancy swanky restaurant. Toasting to friends with that cheesy laugh or that wink and the gun shit. Lol. Then heading to some jazz spot to dance. Somehow at age 35, my imagination is still as vivid as ever!

Whatever don't judge me.

By the time I made it to the light right in front of the Varsity, IT happened.

Melissa and I are talking about how crazy things can get downtown in traffic, and crash!! Bang! ¥¡¡©®!

Some freaking kid. Texting and driving, looking down and smoking rear ended me with a rider in my back seat!

My first response was Melissa, are you ok? Melissa responded quickly, "Yeah, I'm alright". "You?"

Just as I responded back the unbelievable happens. The plot gets thicker.

Squealing tires, burning rubber. SKKKKEEEEEQQ!

Our little rear-ender has sped around a few cars and is down the street about to make a break onto the expressway!

Only problem is that there are a few obstacles in his way that I can see right off the top.

First things first. The car is an older Honda probably a 99-2000 Honda Accord. I could tell from the sluggish speed the car was hardly capable of its best performance abilities and this fact was being proven to our hit-n-runner, as well.

At least that's what his eyes said as I caught a glimpse of them in the side mirror during his soon to-be failed attempt as a getaway.

All I was thinking at this point was 'This is crazy!' I have a rider in the back seat, and we have just been involved in a Hit-N-Run!

Now because I'm built this way, I can't just let this little punk hit my ride and speed off like nothing happened.

OH, HELL NO!! My Spidey senses kick in and...

"Yup, you is motherfuckn right." (In my 2Chainz voice), I say fuck it. We're in high pursuit.

I can see the Honda cutting thru the Varsity parking deck from the back headed towards Spring Street.

I speed up and we're right on his tail!

I'm cutting thru the parking deck fast, disregarding the many speedbumps that slow my pursuit.

The young driver doesn't seem to be phased by the speed bumps either. He's flying high without a care! WTF!!

Until he realizes his 2nd problem. Lol.

Spring Street is a one-way.

I'm cutting through the parking lot and honking long and loud. Making a TOTAL scene.

I cut over by the south exit of the parking lot by Spring Street.

Got 'em cornered! Screech.!!!!

Now that I've got him cornered my mind wonders. I'm hoping buddy doesn't try to take off again as I get out of my car. I would have totally had to clip 'em.

Besides, I think I've seen enough Bad Boys and Fast N Furious movies to get the job done.

Thankfully, the kid stops the car and my saner mind prevailed.

I hop out of the car. All I say is kid WTF??!

What is your problem?

I have a million questions for the kid as he gets out of his vehicle. To start, do you know you could've hurt people?? Why did you speed off like that??

The kid says nothing just stands there looking like a deer in headlights.

I know a sista has the ability to apply pressure but pull it together. If you have the balls to run, you should have the balls to face the consequences.

In my past life I would have been all over this fool like a fat man in some tight draws. No matter his age. My motto was like the comedic genius Mr. Richard Pryor always said, "It don't matter, if you cross me you can get it. From ages 8 to 80. Blind, crippled, or crazy".

However now that I am an adult.

I can handle things with dignity and a calm and rational mind.

Sometimes.

When the kid gets out of the car, he stands about 5'9. He's slim with glasses and a skull cap that fits like a beanie on his head, just covering a field of dark curly locks. Kid couldn't weigh more than a buck 20-30, at best. His eye's looked big. Like he was just as shook-up as the rest of us. Meghan and I, I mean.

His hands were shaking, and his mouth appeared as if it were dry.

"Ma'am, I am so sorry."

There was a white ring of dryness around his lips, that housed flaky cracked layers that were peeling profusely due to the dry chill in the air this winter.

Again, he says, "Ma'am I'm sorry."

"I sped off because I'm not supposed to be out of the house right now. I'm grounded, and my dad said I couldn't use the car anymore".

Oh yeah, is my only response as junior spills his heart out in the Varsity parking deck. He goes on to say he was just in a wreck 2 weeks ago!

Ah, ha! Finally, some valid answers from this kid. Hence BIG DADDY'S reason for punishment in the first place I'm sure.

Damn kid, you can't catch a break! I'm about to call your pops too.

But before the festivities I had to apply a little more pressure and shake the kid down really quick. I want to get a picture of his real ID, address etc. Then I can get his dad's info.

Let's face it this kid's track record is beyond shaky. Enough with the trickery. I don't know you man, SAME TIME. Ended up making the kid call his dad from his own cell phone.

After a quick chat with dad he assures me that if there are any damages Amil will be handling them. He asked me to please call him back with any details.

In the end, there is no major damage to my vehicle. I still have a rider and I must get back to work! I don't have any more time to lecture junior. I already called his dad and confirmed his whereabouts. I went ahead and set junior free.

Melissa and I had a good laugh on the way to her destination.

PRO DRIVER TIP 3

Pick a schedule and hold yourself to it.
Accountability.
Is all in your hands!!

CHAPTER FOUR

THE SINGING SEEING EYE DOG

Pickup Location: The Vortex
Five Points: Atlanta GA
Time: 7:48 PM

It's raining downtown in the A today. I just got on the road 15 minutes ago and I have received four calls already because of a rider downtown with a seeing eye dog that NO-ONE, (Uber Driver I mean) wants to pick up. Five drivers have refused this rider and he happens to be legit blind and needs the seeing eye dog to get around.

Now I'm faced with life's moral decisions and it doesn't take me long to make the call.

Alright, I'll bite.

Mike from Uber Corporate gave me a call, trying to finesse the situation, I guess.

I'll pick the guy and his dog up, I replied to Mike over the phone. Send me his contact info and his location please sir.

Mike had been the one who called from the Uber field office to let me know the bad luck our seeing impaired friend was having flagging down a ride. Turns out I was call number 7!

Alright! Alright! I won't shoot the messenger this time, Mike. Lol.

But really, how bad could it be? I thought to myself. The guy is blind. Have a little compassion people!

Geesh, this sure is a tough crowd.

Got the info, dialed the rider. His name is Howard.

Ring, ring.

Hello, Howard my name is Nico I'm gonna be your Uber driver tonight. What is your location?

Howard replied, "I'm at the Vortex."

I smiled and said, I know the spot be there in 5, and I'm on my way for pickup.

Thank goodness I was over by Zoo Atlanta really close to the old Fourth Ward.

The Vortex is a well-known restaurant in Little Five Points. Always featured in food magazines like Zagat and Food Network. The Vortex has a sign you can't forget. The "O" in the word Vortex looks like a never-ending spiral line shaped like an" O". I ate there a few times. A true landmark and THE BURGERS are to die for!

Told Howard my famous one liner, "I'm in a silver Chevy, tinted windows". That's how I always describe my car to riders. I told him I would turn my hazards on but not even sure if that information would be helpful in this instance. I'll just find him. Shouldn't be hard to find a blind guy and a seeing eye dog in the rain in front of the Vortex.

Don't overthink this Nico is all my mind can possess. Chill.

The rain has me feeling calm. However, Atlanta drivers have a way of ruining that "Good Vibe" feeling. Maybe it's their poor decision- making skills that make people drive extra reckless when it rains. But 2che.

I need music. Today is Dave Matthews all the way. Yeah, I said Dave Matthews.

Let's start with a little "Ants Marching". Set the mood, feeling good.

I'm up the street now and I can see the red Vortex sign ahead. The eyes of the Vortex sign look like a never-ending maze and its site is familiar. Homey even comforting.

No dog yet. I pass the light and make a left into the parking lot.

HOLY SHIT! That is a big ass dog!

More like a seeing eye DINOSAUR. Not just a seeing eye dog!!

HELLO?! The reality of this situation is that I drive a Sedan!

Damn, I totally want to cancel this ride!

Nope, don't do it! My conscious yells out, don't do it! You gave your word, and this guy has been having a rough day. Just give the ride and go to the car wash afterward are my thoughts immediately.

Fine. Composure set.

The parking lot is full of cars, and there looks like a group of people standing by the lot attendant with umbrellas in the middle of the crowded parking lot. I pull up right in front of the people and I stop the car.

The back-door swings open first.

"Hey, I'm Howard and this sweet guy is "Billy.""

I have a blanket for Billy, Howard says. He lays the blanket down in the back seat and say, "Trust me, he's harmless."

I said okay slowly. I love dogs I have two at home myself.

Hi Billy, I said and rubbed the "big guys" head.

Howard closes the back door and hops in the front. He seems to be getting around REALLY well for a blind guy, from what I can see.

Thanks again for picking us up Howard says.

We have been waiting on someone to accept our ride for over an hour now! The valet guys were so nice to us. They let Billy and I stand under their tent in the rain.

I'm thinking yeah, Billy is quite the silent intimidator. But I replied, there's still good people out there, eh Howard?

Yes, I guess there are, Howard concurred.

So, where are you guys headed? Is the address correct in the app? Howard sounded off, 'we are literally going 10 minutes away'.

Damn, another short trip I thought. Oh well, the nights young.

Then I turn up the tunes a little bit. Dave Matthews in this moment is singing my favorite part of the song, where he kind of speaks in tongues. It's almost like Dave is shouting or having a spiritual moment. You can hardly make out any words he says but the energy and rhythm are still very much in tune.

It goes "We all do it the same wayyyyyyyy yeah", "Candyman tempting the thoughts of a sweet tooth tortured by weight loss program cutting the corners Loose end, loose end, cut, cut…. Take these chances".

All of a sudden Billy sits up in the back seat and begins to howl the song. "HOOOOOOwwwwww, EEEEERRRRRR" perfectly on time with the chorus part of the song.

Wow! I'm impressed I said to Howard. Is he singing??

"Ha, Ha, Ha" cried Howard.

Yes! This is Billy's favorite song! He always sings to Dave Matthews.

And sure enough, every time Dave hits the hook, "They all do it the same wayyyyyy, yeah", "BAARRRROOOO!"

There goes Billy.

This is priceless. A singing seeing eye dog!

Awesome.

You guys should be in show business!!

Howard, have you ever thought about sharing Billy with the rest of the world?

Does Billy sing to any other songs?

Howard said ironically, Billy only sings to Dave Matthews and The Rolling Stones.

But who knows what other music will inspire Billy to cultivate his musical stylings in the future?

Howard and I get another chuckle in between the two of us before we part ways.

GPS sounds off. In 1000 ft your destination will be on the left.

"Pull up behind this blue truck in front of the third house on the left" Howard says.

"Perfect, thanks. It was so nice meeting you Nico. Thanks, so much for the ride. "C'mon Billy, we're home".

Hope to see you guys again. Take care.

As I pull off, I realize I love this gig! You just never know...

Cool ride.

PRO DRIVER TIP 4

Know when to fold 'em!
9x's outta 10, if a person is so drunk, they're belligerent and throwing up when you arrive….
Things WON'T get better during a 10-15minute ride.
There is a ride cancel button on your UBER app for a reason.

CHAPTER FIVE

PUKERS: Volume 1, 2 and 3

Pick Up Location: Various places that serve alcohol.
Anywhere, Atlanta, GA
Time: Anytime Liquor is being poured.

I decided to keep this chapter as transparent and to the point as possible. Let's face it, when the third motherfucker has thrown up in your back seat. It's just as elegant and memorable as the first. So, I decided to include all three experiences, so we can acknowledge that shit exists without giving to much 'power to' or 'glorifying' the act in itself.

Each time I've had a puker the rider ironically came from the same general vicinity for pickup as the first. The Buckhead area, or Virginia Highlands.

The combination of college students, booze and zero limitations are scary as shit to a sane sober adult.

Keyword, ADULT!

Set some limits.

Know what your limit feels like, that's the key. Taking that last shot beyond your limit brings the puke. No other conclusion.

The third puker was accompanied by two sober friends. Her friends clearly didn't give a damn about her because they both paid more attention to their phones than their drunk friend fading in and out of consciousness!

The chunks happened after the car stopped at their drop off location. An apartment complex in Roswell.

Motion sometimes is the worst decision you'll ever make when your drunk. As soon as the car is in park, I hear that awful regurgitating sound.

My neck does a 360 QUICK

I know this chick is not throwing up in my car!

Indeed, she was.

Funny part is she tried to clean up her chunks with a paper towel she pulled out from her purse!

My thought was, why the fuck didn't you puke in the purse?

In reality I said Bitch, get out!

Because at the end of the day, a paper towel won't remove the grossness of puke in the fabric of your carpet and seat cushions. Customers still must sit back there and endure a smelly ride, and people don't tend to like to ride in stinky, puke filled Ubers.

Clearly the car must be taken off the road to get detailed, aired out, carpets cleaned etc. That means NO Revenue.

What a bummer.

Still, I have to do my due diligence.

Next I pull over and take pics to send to Uber. This is how I get my cleaning fee. Definitely a must do.

When I complete the pics and description on the Uber app, I immediately get offline.

Lights out ATL.

Damnit!

PRO DRIVER TIP 5

Generally speaking. In the famous words of
Maya Angelou, 'When a person tells you who
they are,
BELIEVE THEM'.
That goes for everybody, PERIOD.
Nuff said.

CHAPTER SIX

66YEAR OLD GROUPIE

Pickup Location: Sweetwater Brewery
NE Atlanta, GA
Time: 8:18 PM

Starting on time tonight even though it's cold." It's the month of December and traffics a bit crazier than usual. Everyone seems to be off work getting some last-minute shopping in. Just making traffic a nightmare!

Did I mention IT'S COLD OUT HERE!!

I'm gonna stop at QuikTrip tonight before I get started. Fuel is filled up, but no hot chocolate in the holder.

Tonight, I'm feeling some "Happy Rap" lol. Time for some old skool music so my trusty Run DMC mix tape feels in order. I like to get my faves in, especially in my travel time to a certain destination. You never really know how far a ride will be so you might as well set the mood just right.

All is how it should be. Now all I need is a tall hot cup of cocoa and the last buttery croissant in that plexi glass case in front of me. QT, always open. Always got the snacks! My fave.

Now, let's get rolln.

Push my money button and I get a rider on the hook immediately. Beep, beep, beep. 6 minutes out. I'll take that!

Rider's name is Terri and she is standing out front the text says. This location is close, and these places tend to be quite crowded this time of night. I think I'll call Terri and get a head start on things.

Ring. Ring. Hi Terri, it's Nico, how are ya? I'm your Uber driver and I'll be arriving in less than 4 minutes. You're at Sweet Water Brewery in Midtown, right?

"Yes, I am" Terri sounded off loudly with a raspy voice.

"I'm wearing a black leather vest and hat with black boots with silver spurs on the back. you can't miss me. "I'm drunk as hell and I need to lie down for a while. So, sweetheart, you can't get here fast enough!"

Yes ma'am, I'll be pulling in straight away! I'll go ahead and stay on the phone with you until I arrive.

Looking at my GPS I am less than 2 minutes away now.

Ms. Terri? Are you still with me?

"Yes, darling I'm still here".

I'm turning on Monroe right now. So, arrival is literally a minute away.

Always take a quick look around the car for anything undesirable. I.E. trash, drinks, items or dirt left behind by previous riders.

Everything's all good.

You never know who your gonna pick up. Treat every rider like royalty and your chances of picking up royalty increases.

I'm gonna change my playlist to some old classic rock. From the sound of Terri, I'm sure she can appreciate some classic rock tunes.

A cool song plays and it's my man Mick…. Please allow me to introduce myself. I'm a man of wealth and taste. Mick Jagger, Rolling Stones is coming out of my speakers. One of my favorite Rolling Stones songs.

As I enter the front gates of the brewery my mind begins to ponder, I'm thinking… Damn, this place is big! They must REALLY make beer here. It sure is big enough to be a brewery. Look at all the people!

I'm turning on Ollie now Ms. Terri. Pulling into the front area where parking is to the left. Can you see me?

As soon as I threw the car in park the back doors swing open. Three people try to get in the car!

Hey everybody!! I'm looking for Terri. Nope, no Terri.

I looked across the courtyard at some benches. There is a woman that fits Terri's description. The woman was wearing a black leather vest and boots with silver spurs on the back. That's' my Terri!

I cleared my throat. Ms. Terri, I'm here, cross the courtyard looking at ya sweetie. Silver car with the hazards on, Come 'on over.

"Okay dear, I'm coming. Slowly, but surely".

She was a woman older in age with dyed blonde hair and a leather purse to match her boots. Black sweater with stones across her chest from the strap of her purse that was perfectly rested by her hip as she stood from the bench and began walking across the courtyard.

Before she reached the door handle, she took the last drag of a cigarette with ashes down to the butt in her mouth. She threw the cigarette butt to the ground. I could hear the spurs spin on the boots as she stepped on the cigarette butt outside the door.

"Whew, thanks for waiting sweetie. I'm Terri".

Hey Terri! I'm Nicole, but most people just call me Nico.

"Nice name Nico, it fits you".

Surprisingly enough for me Terri knew the city pretty well. She had her own special route she wanted me to follow to get her to the CNN building downtown where the hotel was.

Terri had her special route already in progress on her phone, so she handed it to me and said, "Follow this please".

No worries I replied. A bit of traffic on I85, gives us some additional time to talk. Terri's interesting, I thought to myself.

She says she is in town for a concert. She's a native of South Carolina. Where she still lives today and has a farm and own's a local restaurant called Blue Oyster. Ironically the same name of the band Ms. Terri, was in town to see.

Hmm, interesting as well.

I really took an interest in Terri's occupation because in my past life I was a restaurant and travel plaza general manager. I totally respect anyone who can withstand the grueling life of service. It takes a special kind of person in my opinion.

Now because of my militant mind frame and my interest in agriculture (or living off the land, so they say); I asked Terri what type of animals she'd raised on her farm?

She replied "cows". "Both cattle and dairy cows. As well as pigs, chickens, goats and horses."

Wow!! That sounds like a full-time job to me!

Terri says, 'It keeps the family busy. By family I mean family trainers and stable jockeys that keep this place running tip top!'. "Honey at my age, I couldn't keep a farm running by myself, even if it were 48hrs in a day!" Ha, ha-ha!!

You're a hoot Ms. Terri! It must feel good to have such a great life.? What got you interested in the restaurant business?

"Well sweetie, it's really more like a sports bar than a restaurant. But still in the same I've been loving Blue Oyster since birth! I got the idea of a sports bar from my dad. He owned the local diner when I was growing up. So, food has always been a part of my life, personally and professionally''.

Terri said her dad always said "When you mix sports, drinks and good food. People will come". Everybody likes a drink.

I had to name the bar Blue Oyster because...

In 500 ft turn left, and your destination will be on the right. GPS sounds off.

I'm sorry Ms. Terri you were saying the reason you had to call your bar Blue Oyster is because?

"Oh yes, my dear. I've only been a huge groupie and followed this band for over 45 years! I mean I have been to every concert. I own every record. I have personally gotten drunk on the tour bus with this band. Even woke up hung over on the tour bus after sleeping with one of the band members of Blue Oyster Band!

Child that was way back when I was young and wild!".

Terri was sure to have pointed that out!

My response was, I'm sure you haven't changed much Ms. Terri.

Ms. Terri wasn't your typical 60+ year old woman. She was youthful and vibrant. More so of someone my age. I had just turned 30!

GPS sounds off arrival in 1000 feet.

This is your stop Ms. Terri

It has been an absolute pleasure having you as a rider. Please accept one of my business cards. I do private rides as well. So, the next time you're in Atlanta and need an Uber, I'll be happy to pick you up!

"Thank you, Nico! The pleasure has been all mine, my dear. Please take my business card and look me up if your ever in the Carolina's. I'd love to treat yourself and your family to dinner"."

Drive safely and please take this $."

Terri says, "Shame on Uber for not having a tip option", "That's why I usually use lyft. Better cars usually and you can tip. You'll be getting 5 stars from me sweetie. Awesome ride Nico take care."

PRO DRIVER TIP 6

Don't be afraid to protect your property.
It's your constitutional right.
Besides,
Who else is going to do it?

CHAPTER SEVEN

HARTSFIELD JACKSON AIRPORT

Pickup Location: 6000 N. Terminal Pkwy
Atlanta, Ga 30320
Time: Anytime of Night

Atlanta Hartsfield Jackson Airport.

Literally one of the largest airports in the world. Plus, we have an International Airport, where all the international flights take place. Just that side alone is literally the size of a small town!

Things can get tricky at the airport. Most of the time APD is directing traffic with a whistle in the middle of the road. Pushing traffic in the direction you DON'T want to go in.

There is major bumper to bumper traffic and people everywhere, so don't think it's just gonna be a breeze to drop someone off or pick someone up at Hartsfield Jackson!

When it comes to direction, forget about it. Your sanity will be tested.

Especially because it seems like a trend almost when it comes to Uber riders. Just about every other airport rider says to me "the direction you're going in right now isn't the right side for my airline". Or I thought I was at the south terminal??...and round and round you'll go.

When reality is; there are only two decisions to be made on the domestic side of Hartsfield Jackson Airport. You must choose Delta, or everybody else!

Why is this so complicated?

Please, let's get with the program people.

Personally, the best approach for me at the airport is definitely a leisurely wait in the "cell phone lot". Either you'll get a "true ride". Which is what I call anything greater than $20 fare. Or you'll be in the waiting room so to speak. Waiting on a true ride to come.

This is the only spot at the airport that has parking with no wait limit. Shit a safe haven to gather your spirit, recompose after a ride before a ride etc.

Literally, the only place at the airport that Atlanta PD won't harass you!

For real. I've seen Atlanta PD find a brotha under a rock and brought his ass out in handcuffs! It can be a scary place if you don't govern yourself accordingly. "I jus sayin ju gottwo look ou fo yusef." (This is a classic quote from the movie Shaft with da homie Samuel L. Jackson).

So many airport rides, I'm not sure where to start. Countless execs busy and on their cell phones the whole ride. Some people are so excited on a Friday night to get home they talk the entire damn ride. Then of course we have the in betweenners; who in my opinion are the absolute best. Because the rider/driver experience is still super memorable. We both know some cool facts about each other probably having a good music experience vibe. Always gonna be comfortable in my ride and my ears aren't bleeding by the time I drop off the rider. Win, win.

I'm sure you already get the gist of things.

The most memorable is another story, altogether.

I remember grinding hard that week. Since Wednesday I've been staying on the rideshare app from late night to early morning rush hour. Building up the bank.

By now it's the but crack of dawn on a Saturday morning. An early morning ride, on a rainy day that ironically was the last ride of my shift. One of those nights that I started my first ride and ended my last ride at the same stop. The airport.

Small rides all night and 'boy I tell ya' a whole lot of em to make the nights quota.

Accountability and motivation are key I have to commit a certain number of hours per week to meet my $number. Homelife is the only motivation needed. I love my life it's beautiful. Abundantly surrounded with beautiful things. I'm favored. Most of all, grateful.

Come what come may.

6am is my quitting time I figure the morning work crowd would start around that time and the way my patience is set up. We should make different arrangements.

The previous rider left me in the Marietta, Roswell area at around 5:08am. It's still dark and I get a rider about 6 miles out. I accept. It's like this at this hour usually, it isn't uncommon to get a ride so far out. I can get a rider 10-15 miles out. If I accept it and want to be a road warrior that night is mostly what that depends on.

Not this time guys. This rider Bill is gonna be that white towel for me tonight.

I went ahead and bussed a U-turn and head south on Roswell Road. The GPS sounds "Head south, you should reach our destination by 5:16am". It's about five minutes up the road, so at the red light I give the car a quick onceover and remove a water bottle that's sitting in the passenger rear door panel. Clearly this was left behind from the last passenger, glad I looked quick, that could've not been a good impression.

Need some smell good, so I spray a little air freshener. It's black ice spray like the "little trees" black ice fragrance. I get a lot of compliments on the smell.

Almost at the destination I turn into a really nice subdivision. I mean really nice. The house I'm going to is on a hill at the top of this golf course community. Swanky. Let me turn this music down a little, don't seem like the kind of neighborhood that listens to Cardi B at 5:30am.

It's still raining pretty hard, so I pull my car into a circular driveway at the top of the hill before I make the phone call to say I'm outside. As I put my car in park, I see a distorted type image in the driveway.

In reality of course, there is not an image. There is a man and he's standing in the driveway. Wearing a raincoat and a hat. In his hand only a briefcase and a folded umbrella, and a small rollaway carryon luggage sat directly on the ground beside him. His glasses were dripping with water along with his hat; yet he stands un phased by the rain.

It's almost crazy, his appearance that is. Not that I am a judgmental person at all, but when unfolded the scene is a bit peculiar....

Calling an Uber in some dreadful weather, standing outside in the rain to wait for this said Uber. Holding an umbrella in his hand and a metal briefcase; both in which would have been an adequate shield from the rain for the old feller. Very weird scene to roll up to.

In the mien time, the call to the rider isn't necessary.

I get out of the car with my umbrella open and gave the rider a smile.

Can I get your suitcase sir?

"No ma'am. Please get in the car and out of this rain."

I get back in and start the ride. As soon as I do the gentleman takes off his hat and adjust his glasses with a dry towel, I provided for the rider in this rainy Atlanta weather.

I always keep some clean towels/paper towels, an umbrella and a baseball cap in the car just in case. The weather is unpredictable these days. It's better to be prepared with extra stuff than to be getting caught with your pants down.

The gentleman leans over the front seat and reaches out his hand to shake mine as I drove.

"Hi, I'm Bill Martin, thanks so much for the towel. Do you always get out of your car in the rain and help strange men with luggage''?

Ha-ha lol, Martin's got jokes.

No sir I don't, just when I'm on duty.

It looks like we are headed to the Airport, eh?

"Yes, get there as fast as you can".

Okay sir, no problem. Just know that quick will cost extra. It takes effort and concentration to be quick. Not to mention the fact that cops' frown on quick, and I can be faced with a hefty fine.

Still I'm interested, so I ask. How quick are we talking?

Bill leans over and says in my ear.

"Let's put it like this, if you can get there in the next 45 minutes there's a nice off work bonus for ya Nico."

Hmmm, incentive. I like it.

Anytime you want a challenge met call the homie I'm competitive as hell. Pure shit talkn, highly conscious, highly intelligent, and extremely confident woman right here.

Once that beast is awakened. Good luck to you, and yours.

I am Totally capable. I got this.

At that moment I remember sitting up in my seat and feeling like it was time for business. Then I proceeded with a quick mirror adjustment. Let's get to it!

The morning traffic coming through downtown Atlanta can get pretty crazy. One hiccup and you could be faced with a standstill of dead traffic that will typically add another 30 min to your trip! You'll look up and you'll be right in that sweet spot downtown where all the expressways meet. Damn.

Can't even describe the congestion in this spot of town. Like not even if I tried. No matter the time, no matter the day. No matter the car, no matter the person driving. Chaos traffic, always. Except this morning. When I tell you Martin and I hit downtown Atlanta and blew through the city like a strong gust of wind.

It seemed like as soon as we got onto the I85 loop to ride into Atlanta Hartsfield, somebody turned the lights on, and everybody WOKE UP!

Wow, plenty of lights up here Mr. Martin. Just when we thought we were the only people awake.

Aye Mr. Martin?! What terminal do you need to be in sir?

North terminal dear I'm flying Delta. Any door is fine on that side.

All I said was 10-4.

Surprisingly with all the lights we still were able to make it to the north terminal door 3 in about fifteen minutes flat from the Sylvan Road exit on I85. Pretty impressive if I say so myself. Made the deadline.

It's still raining. So, I make sure I park close to the curb for easy access to a covering to shield my rider a bit from the rain. Even though the weather is less than elegant, service should never suffer. Service should always be 5 stars.

As I put my car in park and throw on my hazards, I reach over to get the umbrella from the passenger side seat beside me. I hopped out of the car to escort Bill with my umbrella and thru the window I notice he is fumbling thru his wallet. I went ahead and grabbed the suitcase from the back to give him a minute.

By the time I grabbed the bag he was stepping out the car with the briefcase. I put the umbrella over Bill and walked him to the front door. He thanked me for the great service, shook my hand and handed me a tip. I thanked Bill for being a great ride.

Running back to the car in the rain distracted me to a point that I had already pulled off and started heading home by the time I realized that the tip Mr. Martin laid on me was a $100 bill. SWEET way to end the day.

Lights out ATL.

.

PRO DRIVER TIP 7

If there are too many people to sit
comfortably and everyone doesn't have access
to a seatbelt, don't do it!
Cmm, Hmm.
Clearing my throat….
It's Ga Law.
Cancel the ride and suggest the group split up or
call an Uber XL.
The penalty and ticket price for over occupancy
is a hefty $350 bucks in GA.
An uber ride up the road makes you about $8
bucks.
Which one makes more of an impact on your
wallet?

CHAPTER EIGHT

FIRST WEEK OF UBER POOL

Pickup Location: Tattletale Lounge
2075 Piedmont Rd.
Time: 2:31 AM

When I got the memo about the changes coming in the week ahead, I was a bit undecided on how I felt about the whole integration for a cheaper ride thing. But the days and the seasons change without us being ready. Friday comes and because I am a mere laborer not the owner of UBER who signs off on all decisions. I decided to play the game a while longer, put on my winner face. IT'S SHOWTIME!!

First interesting Uber Pool pickup for me was right in Buckhead.

Old Man...Check. Strip Club...Check. The damn butt crack of dawn... Check.

The last rider was dropped off at the same location. That rarely happens. Tattletales must be popular tonight.

The app chimes as soon as I end my last ride. The riders name is Don. This guy is super boozed up.

He swings open the door and makes a loud noise as he sits down hard in the back seat.

"Hey there, how are we doing?"

I always speak as a rider enters, its courteous. Don, "The Old Man", (which is how we will refer to Don for the rest of this chapter. Just because I believe if we give him a name, he becomes human, and this guy was less than that, believe me).

The old man replies, "I'm past my bedtime baby. Now I just need something warm, young and soft to curl up next to".

I quickly responded with, "No luck in the strip club"??

Old man says, "No baby, but the night is young". Ha, Ha, Ha. Laughing like an old creep and looking like one too. Eeewww!!

He's a white male, age 60-70 years, grey hair dyed blonde in some areas. He wore black jeans, biker boots, a grey colored tee shirt with apparent grease stains that read "SUPER FREAK".

The piece de resistance was a greasy bandana to cover up the receded hairline our Casanova here is dying to go unnoticed.

He reeks of an unpleasant aroma of booze, sweaty ass, old spice, grease and old wet cigarettes. I'm sure all roads lead to that dumpster of a mouth for the culprit of the foul odors.

Very funny, I responded.

The App sounds off. Change route in progress.

"Just got another rider, hold on, gotta make a U- turn.

After I turn around, we are headed south, now. Only 4 minutes to my next destination, Cyan on Peachtree.

Before I knew it GPS sounds "In 500 feet your destination is on the right. 'Ding, "You have arrived".

I pulled up just past the entrance and the front door swings open. A young lady no more than 20-21 years old about 5'3 and 115 lbs., says slowly,

"I'm Emily. I'm so glad you're here! I am ready to go home! Two other drivers cancelled on me!"

My mommy instincts kick in when I heard that. I gave Emily my coat and a cold water to sip on, she looks a bit shaken up. Although I am feeling like a protector up front, we still have the old man in the back seat. I decided that I won't get personal with Emily. We have seedy characters among us. I just said "Oh sweetie! I'm so sorry that happened to you. I'm here now, Let's get you home safe. Buckle up!

All set let's go! GPS says loudly. About 14 min to your destination. The app just calculates the closest ride, from the last pickup I'm assuming. As the driver, you have no idea who you're dropping off first.

The mysteries with the infamous "Uber pool" option continue. Which, by the way in my opinion sucks ass!

Sometimes human judgement in certain situations is necessary. Not just a matter of distance.

In any event, let me fine tune the music and offer a bottled water to my passengers is my next minds thought.

The geezer interjects. "So, Emily", the old man says, in this creepy, dirty old man way.

What did you do with yourself tonight baby?

Emily replied quickly.

"Nothing really, I just hung out with some cool friends I met at the beach in Miami.", "they're in town for the weekend".

Old man says, HMMM, so ya'll are a couple of cuties eh? HA, HA, HA

Emily replies, "I suppose so." "Where are you coming from this late?"

Old man smirks and says the 'strip club'. All I was thinking is I'm just glad his ass didn't lie and say some ridiculous bullshit like,' Church'.

He totally hesitated with the next response and looked at my eyes in the rear-view mirror for confirmation. Hell, 'YES', I'll bust ya old ass out in a lie if you had the balls to tell one!

I'm totally ear hustling at this point, but who cares?

I know I don't give a damn. His rusty tail is trying to be fresh and he could easily be both mine and Emily's granddaddy, with no worries at ALL!

Emily didn't seem too impressed with the strip club answer, so she decided to get involved with candy crush the remainder of the ride home.

Hallelujah, candy crush.

Two minutes till destination and Emily says, "Okay this is me." This is my neighborhood. After this stop sign take the next right and you can just pull up behind this truck."

Damn I hated the fact that we came to her stop first.

Old man says, "WOW nice house!"

I interject with, "Have a good night Emily" and I begin to put the car in reverse and head to Geezer Land.

Emily runs up the driveway waving goodbye, such a sweet young lady.

Old man rolls the window down to keep staring at Emily as I drove off. What a pervert!

So, I put the child safety window lock on. If fresh air is what the geezer wants…. I'll do much to oblige.

Seriously though. What if this old bastard comes back to pay Emily a much more personal visit? Totally uncomfortable with shit like that! Yet and still, there has been no crime committed, technically. But what about the moral cops? The times you wish you could be a mind reader. Just for a mere gut check confirmation.

Rerouting…. Ok all set, Let's Go! GPS sounds again. About 20 minutes out I screamed over the loud wind, whipping through the back seat where the old man is trying to get a few winks of shut eye. But to No Avail.

Small talk is to a bone minimum. I'm sure with the child lock on the window and all the dry remarks, grandpa here is totally feeling my energy. I can only be described as a person who is unafraid of expression. I believe you can lack imagination and still be able to attune to my station, in other words.

In 1000 ft you will reach your destination, GPS sounds off. Old man yawns and says, "Pull up in the second driveway thanks. I'm the second townhouse on the left. Brick. I love brick. Thanks for the ride."

I turn the car around in the cul-de-sac and take a good look at this guy walking into his house. I'll go once I get this guy address and tag information from the dirty van in his driveway.

I'm going to go ahead and put this info in my little black book of creeps for future cross reference.

PRO DRIVER TIP 8

Think outside the box.
Weather is unpredictable.
As a rideshare driver
Your car is your second home on wheels!
You're a road warrior, have the necessities.

CHAPTER NINE

IT'S A GIRL

Pickup Location: Magnolia Chase Apartments
Decatur, GA
Time: 3:36 AM

Wow, it's been a rough night! I started early because it's Wednesday and today starts my driving week. I usually hit the road at about seven or eight on days like this. So, by this time, you can forget it buddy. I'm ready to throw the ole' hat in.

It's about 3:30 am, so I'm feeling like it's time to retire. Decision made. Last ride for sure.

Turn on the app and it takes quite a while to get a ride. Over 10 minutes. Just as I was about to give up and call it quits, I get a request. Beep, Beep, Beep……. Accept.

GPS sounds. Make a U-Turn. I turn around, damn I just passed this place.

Its late, and it's a single rider. NOTE: Always call the rider.

Ring, ring.

"Hello, I'm outside the apartments at the top of the hill. I am wearing a brown jacket", said a sweet Latin voice with a heavy accent on the other end of my phone.

I responded with "Yes, ma'am, I'm turning around now. Be there in 2 minutes".

When I arrived, at the top of the hill a small woman leaning on a tree at the top of the hill holding her stomach and what appears to be an overnight bag. The small Latin woman has long curly brown hair, about shoulder length and she's wearing it back in a ponytail.

As I pull into a spot in front of the passenger my headlights reflect her face as a spotlight would on the Maestro of music.

On her face is gut wrenching pain, as she breathes very quickly and grips her stomach to confirm the pain. I throw the car in park and jump out frantically.

OH, my goodness, you ok?

"NO", she says, "I am having contractions and I need to go to Northside Hospital, as fast as you can!"

I responded with I can see that. Let's get you seated in the back seat.

I open the door and put mommy-to- be safely in the back seat with a double buckle up for safety. I throw the bag on the other side and jump back into the car.

I'm nervous. Adrenaline has clearly taken over because I'm already out of the apartment complex when I realize I don't have the GPS on!

I gotta gain my composure and figure out where we are going, so fast.

My mind is racing even faster. GPS takes us to the hospital. I'm thinking, what a night! The rundown is ridiculous right now. Just moments ago, I decided this is my last ride. I pull up to a woman in a brown coat and a humungous bump under the coat. She's carrying a large black bag. I notice she is engaged in some heavy Lamaze type breathing.

Is everything okay ma'am is naturally my response. But Holy Shit!

I don't know a damn thing about giving birth! Only what I've seen in movies, and I'm sure that shit has been watered down, to say the least.

If I keep going on like this I can only imagine where my mind will end up. Gotta get refocused.

No time to think. Tire's squealing, and we're rolling fast with our sights on Northside Hospital.

Damn. GPS says 12 minutes out.

Do you know what can happen in 12 minutes?! A baby! That's what!

Alright, a brief second talk with myself. "Self! Pull it together!", end quote.

I need to stop panicking.

I roll my window down and listen to the street. It always seems to calm me.

My next thought was it would probably be a good idea to be able to see the rider's face because I couldn't always make out clearly what she was saying. I adjust my rearview mirror and at that moment, our eyes lock.

Ma'am. I'm not trying to be all up in your business or anything. But why did you call an Uber, and not an ambulance?

The young lady replied, "I don't have insurance, and an ambulance is very expensive".

Hmm, I thought. Good thinking.

Then the woman said in between breathing, "By the way, my name is Maria".

Alright, Maria. Keep breathing my dear. 8 minutes till arrival. Hee, hee, hoooo. Hee, hee, hooo. Great job Maria!

Hey Maria, do you mind if I turn on the music? They say it soothes the baby if you play music.

As soon as the radio comes on its V-103. Maria says she likes this station, so we will keep it here. Whatever works! It's the "Quiet Storm", one of my favorite radio times and what do you know it's Tamia. "Officially Missing U", love this track.

Yeah, Maria this is what we need. A little road music to set the tone. Of course, what I'm really thinking is, I know you do like this quiet storm music. Baby making music is more like it. You would think you would've had enough. My goodness woman, that's why you're in the situation you're in!

Hee, hee, hoooo. Hee, hee, hoooo. Keep breathing Maria we're almost there.

Maria screams, "Oh My God!" "My water just broke."

Wow. I never heard that before.

It's ok, everything is ok! Keep breathing Maria. We are about to pull into emergency.

Bump, bump, screech. Tires squealing again as we arrived in the emergency ambulance driveway up front.

Just keep breathing deep, your doing so well Maria. Just keep breathing, and I'll be right back, I'm about to go get a wheelchair.

Running back to Maria with the wheelchair and a nurse that I just grabbed at the nurse's station.

As promised, I came back for you.

I said to Maria joking to make her smile. Helping Maria hold her balance, the nurse and I slide Maria into the wheelchair.

Still in a panic I run behind the wheelchair as the nurse is rolling Maria into the Maternity Ward. Maria is mumbling something.

I get closer to hear her better.

"Bag"

She says it again, "bag."

I hand Maria off to the nurse and run back to the car to get the bag. By the time I get back with the bag, I see no one. No nurse, no Maria.

The waiting area receptionist isn't much help in a crisis either. Now I'm sitting in the waiting area. Its late and I still have the bag.

Leave it up front or wait to see how things go with Maria?

Seeing as though it's well after 4am now and my back seat is soaked. I may as well park and get a conclusion to my action for the night.

Besides, I'm a sucker for a sobbed story.

As I sit in the emergency waiting room, I realized something. There are other miracles happening right now too.

5:41am Sophia Angelica Sanchez born 7lbs 8oz.

PRO DRIVER TIP 9

Be sure to have the appropriate
accommodations and refreshments.
iPhone chargers, water, mints and a smile.
You never know who your picking up!

CHAPTER TEN

CAN'T BUY CLASS

Pickup: Location: Burkhardt's Midtown, Piedmont
Ave
Time: 2:53 AM

Friday night lights!! There's a party out there for everyone. Some of us just don't know when to return home!

Current situation... I've been out all night since around 8pm. Just dropped off a ride at Piedmont Park and at this hour I like to call it the after-club rush hour. This is the time of the night that you just let the app run and see where it takes you. Every ride counts as money. crunch time.

The app chimes again. It's super close to Piedmont Park area, about two blocks up the road. It takes me about 2 min to get there.

I arrive to see all the usual's except the one I'm looking for. The rider!

What I've got is a rider on the app, traffic in the streets, and lots of people standing outside in the parking lot.

Midtown Atlanta, and no one is approaching my car...let's call the rider.

Rider answers, he sounds drunk and I hear loud music.

I holler loudly "This is your Uber Driver, I'm out front, silver Chevy tinted windows. I've got my hazards on, so you can see me."

"Ok we're coming out now."

I look around the car...water, peppermints, car fresh, good music. Check. I contacted the rider, so as far as I'm concerned, we are a go for a good ride.

Time is moving. I've already been waiting 5 minutes. I'll wait. 2:58 am, still waiting.

Second call to the rider, no answer this time. Alright two more minutes and I'm calling it quits, I thought to myself. Seconds later the door swings open.

"Are you Nico? I'm Byron and this is my partner Evan. We're just headed up the street to Virginia Highlands".

Ok guys let's roll. I begin the trip and start driving.

Immediately there is loud talking in the back seat. Water anyone? Mints?

"No thanks, this is a really quick ride" Byron says. "Take this right. It's a back-alley shortcut, much quicker".

Ok.

"Pull up in the alley we will get out here".

Alright guys, is there any reason you wouldn't give me a five-star rating? Evan says. "Girl save your breath. Byron NEVER gives a five-star rating, even on a perfect ride like this he'll complain. With his cheap ass, so Uber refunds his ride!!"

OMG, are you serious?

WTF Byron!!

An Uber ride this short is less than 5 bucks!

I blow more than that on the vending machines at an Amusement Park!!

Have a good evening you two.

Doors close, end ride and I quickly rate that jerk a 1 before he ruins my 5 Star driver rating.

Well, I guess you can't buy class. If class was for sale, as a much-needed gift I would've given Byron 5 bucks worth!

PRO DRIVER TIP 10

Keep track of your mileage and gas
consumption.
Sure, receipts get messy to handle.
Just Know that IRS debt gets messier quicker.
Turn this shit into an asset, not a liability.
You are the business owner.

CHAPTER ELEVEN

TAXI DRIVERS HATE ME

Pickup Location: ANYWHERE in Atlanta. Mostly at the airport or any large public place with frequent people traffic.

Time: Evening, Afternoon, Mornings

I say this with confidence and much experience. I have done the research on these guys and let me tell ya. The stats aren't pretty.

On any given day in Atlanta, you will get animosity, so to speak from taxi drivers. Especially the ones in the yellow cabs. The animosity can get very rude and noticeable as well. It's clear they don't give a damn about Uber drivers because they stare as you pass with a decal in your window. A few times for me the stares have turned into something much more sinister. Like a middle finger!

Now what did I do, other than wake up with a better idea than you did??

Don't hate the player partner. Change the game.

I actually had an entire level-headed conversation with a taxi driver on a natural term and found out the basics of why hating Uber drivers is across the board when it comes to taxicab professionals.

Other than the obvious.

The cars that taxi drivers drive most don't own. There is a dollar amount that comes out of the money they collect and it's almost like a rental. Much like UBER if you don't own your ride.

Another difference is the hefty fees taxicab drivers must pay for a license to transport. This fee must be renewed yearly as a fleet. Also, the other individuals you have to pay wages to in a taxi service. Like dispatch, the owner and the driver.

Wow. I guess all that overhead explains why taxi rides are so fucking expensive!

I guess one could feel badly about rideshare companies coming in and dominating an industry of taxicab drivers in a matter of minutes!

But on the other hand, it's a dog eat dog world and if you can't beat em' you should probably join em'.

The reason?

For me it seems less than appropriate that a human would have such animosity for another human that they don't know or have never met.

What gives you the right to judge at all, much less judgement of a stranger.

How does one arrive at such a bias opinion?

Was it a chain of events that make that person so prefixed on this emotion; or was it just the familiarity of the surroundings and a single act of reference?

If there is one thing that is uniform across the globe, it's the fact that when money is involved emotions are heightened. Even if there is no conformation there is still high emotion and intensity even if you think someone makes more money than you. Confirmation isn't necessary.

All the same questions usually arise in the mind of the less profitable.

Like why is her salary more than mine?

Is she better than me?

What is she doing differently?

What makes it work?

Can I change my approach and make more money too?

What does she have that I don't?

Is there a chance for victory from this defeat?

While I over stand the mind frame of someone who feels slighted or mistreated I don't quite over stand envy. If someone else seems to have the recipe for success, ask questions. Get involved so you can see firsthand how that person arrived at the conclusion of success.

However, getting the answers has a quite different approach at times. In my experience I have found that when I have asked my own family for the recipe of success I get turned away, misinformed or left out on the ledge. That's not to say some people don't operate under a different pretense, that's just what I have encountered in MY experience, with MY family.

Family is quick to pass down traditions like religion and holidays etc. What about passing on a trade instead of tradition?

Feed a man and he can eat for a day. Teach a man how to fish and he can eat for a lifetime. Trade over tradition. The new family heirloom.

Ironically in my travels I have had most of the best advice from total strangers.

When I ask a total stranger about the recipe for success; the answer has always been yes, I'd love to share my experience! Along with some solid advice on their past experiences and obstacles that might come into play for my journey ahead.

Ask before envy. Closed mouths will never get fed. You'll be surprised how many people would be willing to help you get ahead.

PRO DRIVER TIP 11

The growing population in Atlanta means more cars, more people. More potholes, more traffic, more gas. More money to be made.
More money to be spent.
Always have some cash set aside for maintenance funds, and make sure its readily available.
This is your business.
If your car isn't on the road, you aren't making any money.

STALKER

Pick up Location: 3707 Roswell Rd
Uptown Apts. Buckhead Atlanta
Time: 1:18 AM

Pickup is about six minutes out from my location right now. The nights still young, I'm keeping a positive outlook on things.

It's a humid muggy night in Atlanta. Peaceful. Noise from the steady flow of cars and a light mist condensation passing my window with light wind that would easily nestle a baby to sleep. I love moving through the city like this.

Minimal noise, minimal people. Just my thoughts, my beats and my riders. Afterall this is a BUSINESS.

It's turning into quite the Thursday night.

So far, all the trips have been long and steady.

Surprisingly tonight I've been all around the city and back. I've had quite a few lengthy rides. Hopefully this will be one too.

Single rider, the app says riders name is Theresa.

Before I could pull into the apartments the phone rings and I'm assuming from the voice it's Theresa, my rider.

"Hello. Press #2880 when you get to the call box out front" "Oh, and how far are you? The app says you're really close."

Yes sweetie. I'm close about to pull in. When I press the code what do I do next?

She said, "Drive all the way up the hill and make the first right. It'll be the second building on the right. I'm coming outside now. I have a backpack and a black outfit on."

Hmm, I thought. I wear all black on the weekends at my security job. No judgement.

Could be everything, could be nothing.

I parked in an empty parking spot in front of the building. Quick check to the backseat for any debris and before I know it, I'm seeing a black catsuit, a black fitted cap and some black Nikes walk down the steps. Pretty face and a pretty large backpack as company.

She walks quickly to the car from the staircase ahead. Gets in the backseat and says, "Hi, I'm Frankie. Nico, I don't have a location set yet because I have two locations".

Okay cool; Frankie, put in the first destination in the app, and when we arrive put in the second destination, and so on. Got it?

Yes, Frankie responded, Got it.

GPS sounds off, destination entered and we're in route to destination 1.

The drive was short, about 8 minutes away from the original location. It's another apartment complex. From the looks of it. Just not very well lit. The apartment building looks like an old motel or extended stay sort of setup.

From the parking lot approaching the building it looks somewhat seedy. Very dark parking lot and the building has a few lights that flicker in the night air as if they might blow like the rest of them.

The cement stairs and iron railings made the outside look cold even in the summer. All the units were in rows and there were two levels that wrapped around the building with matching cement staircases and iron rails.

Frankie seemed very familiar with her surroundings and told me very calmly to pull up on the south side of the building and keep the car running. She grabbed a camera from her backpack and put the bag back on the floor.

She said, "Nico If you hear anything strange or if I don't come back, I left my cell phone in my backpack".

Because I had never heard anyone say that to me unless it was serious. I decided to probe and ask Frankie if I should be worried?

Is everything ok?

She said yes. I'm just going to get a few things I left at my boyfriend's place.

Ok I thought, sounds a little suspicious but harmless enough.

Frankie gets out of the car, walks into a dark spot and disappears almost immediately.

Damn she disappeared quick.

Maybe there's an elevator in this joint after all!

I turned on some music, hopefully Frankie is coming right out like she said.

Note: An Uber driver that's sitting idle waiting on people is NOT making any real coins.

As I look up, I could see Frankie on the top-level walking briskly and traveling to the other side of the building. Hmm, wonder why she had me park all the way over here?? Maybe I'm thinking too much. I have been known to do that from time to time.

Frankie hits a doorway and stops. It looks like she is trying to listen for something. She puts her ear to the door; she touches the doorknob and tries to turn it. No luck.

She starts banging on the door and screaming loud. I can hear her clearly in the car where I sat observing this entire performance. Someone comes to the door and opens it a crack. Apparently, whoever she is yelling at has come to the door to yell back!

I look away.

I look at Facebook on my phone as I'm still able to overhear the battle go on for a few minutes.

I took another glimpse towards the irate rider and can see neighbors looking out of their doors and windows at the scene Frankie and her friend are making.

Being someone who grew up in apartments in an area that was poverty stricken I know a thing or two about tuning some shit out or minding my own business when people are having a disagreement.

Unfortunately, everyone doesn't follow the "house" rules all the time!

They go on yelling for a while. Frankie starts hitting the window and the door with something that looked blunt, dark and large.

In the distance, gaining fast I see two squad cars and they are approaching the building now with lights on. In the dark all the lights look like the 4th of July. Finally, some lights in this place but I wasn't expecting such a commotion in the process, WTH!!

Frankie turns around, sees the cops and the lights but decides she is gonna stay where she is and continue to yell.

This woman is BOLD. With a capital B. Shit at this point Frankie is proving her gangsta status as we speak. (In my eyes at least).

Surly the police aren't coming for her??!!

I'm still sitting and until now I have been okay with the ride. Now it seems that law enforcement is getting involved and this is kinda where I get off. This seems like the fine line I don't anticipate on crossing. Driving a rider to a destination, committing a felony?! Not what I had on my agenda for the day.

As the police exit their vehicles and approach the building, they are engaging Frankie by the name Mrs. Thompson. One cop gets on the bullhorn and says "Mrs. Thompson, It's time to go now. You were here two nights ago. You know there is a restraining order against you, and you are now in violation of said order. Now it's time to stop making all this noise and let these good people get some rest. You and I have a long night ahead of us at the Station".

As he was making the statement the other cop sprints up the stairs and is approaching the top of the staircase where Frankie is. As soon as she sees the cop getting close, Frankie makes a b-line to the backend of the building. Through a breezeway and down the side staircase where I still sat in my car. Because, I'm a dumbass.

At this point I'm just in pure amazement that this is happening.

Frankie swings the passenger side door open, shuts it hard while damn near breaking my window. She reaches in her backpack for her cell phone and says "GO MAN!! GOOO!!!"

Ahhh. NO MA'AM!!

If I pull off from here, we are fugitives from justice! Not on duty. Not on duty.

I put the car in park, grabbed the keys and got the hell out. Let me go ahead and do my civic duties.

Let this fine officer approach the vehicle and reprimand the perp.

She's a Veteran Stalker. WTF!!

PRO DRIVER TIP 12

There's GOLD in them their hills, Sonny!
Surge pricing is the time to gain some
revenue. Go where the money is and if you get
there early.
Then it's just a matter of 'when you're HOT
you're HOT.'
Let's get this $Money!

CHAPTER THIRTEEN

CONFESSIONS

Pickup Location: ALL OVER THE CITY from all
directions North, South, East, West.
Time: Late night, Early mornings

Countless confessions.

Most people know that in this big city. With all these
people. All these rideshare apps and all this traffic. They
will probably NEVER see me again! Most times they
are right about that. It'll probably be a cold day in hell
before you run into the rideshare driver you told about
the lowest point of your existence. Someone you
DON'T know at all, but you felt inclined to tell them
about your lying, cheating, low down, down low,
scheming, stealing, trash mouth moments on a lonely
drunken ride home, in an UBER.

I've been told about affairs by husbands and wives
and by one guy who was a business partner of a husband
and wife team and he was sleeping with both of them!

One guy was feeling so damn bad about things that he
just had to scold himself thru me but all alone.

It was super funny. He starts the confession by asking
me if I knew any people who were dishonest?

Of course, I said yes.

Then he retorted by telling me that the dishonest people I know all rolled up into one wouldn't be on the level of dishonest shit he was up to. He said he was responsible for finances at work and several other places and he was stealing from all of them. He said his main objective was to steal from the people who entrusted him with these responsibilities.

But what if?

What if there was some type of moral code or responsibility you had to possess? What if you couldn't project these poor images or spouge this vomit on strangers? What if displaying bad character to anyone was a crime? UNLESS you were able to add a heaping spoonful onto the plate before you.

Accountability. I personally believe that thinking in this capacity would change the way we build relationships. We would be pushed as a people to have better character or basic principals in life.

As of today, there is no real moral police or even code of ethics among people. Human beings. Which is also funny because even monkeys and all marine life have a code. Their own eco system. A way of doing things that coincides with natures law.

Natures Law. The only law that should be followed and respected here within our reality.

You can't trust everyone.

PRO DRIVER TIP 13

If you take this business seriously there are
multiple streams of income to be made here.
I.E. Referrals, consulting, website hosting, click
-advertisements.
Think smart.

CHAPTER FOURTEEN

HOLY TRINITY

Pickup Location: Buckhead: The Saloon
Time: Weekends, Weekdays, $2 Tuesday

The Holy Trinity happens only with all the right elements are present. In the world of Atlanta there are only a few places you can be for the Holy trinity to take place and pay you handsomely.

Let's break it down so to speak.

What is the Holy Trinity you ask?

It's not the Holy Trinity I'm sure most of you are familiar with. This thing has nothing to do with immaculate conception without a woman or men levitating in the clouds.

The Holy Trinity I am speaking of is a term I have endured during driving Uber. Not to mention the weekends in Atlanta club life are so lit they must be called something!

A chain of events is really what endeared the term.

I remember being super busy on this weekend. Everything that could be a moving part, or a potential situation became one. Every pickup had a situation or a bomb to defuse.

I mean it was such an epic night that two of the stories in this book happened on this very day! True story. Stories in particular; "Two Timer" and "Mom WTF".

But still Nico, you ask? Are you implying that just these two major events are enough to call it the Holy Trinity?

I think not. It's a recipe that's much more sinister I'm afraid.

Drama (just so she doesn't remain nameless) is our first ingredient. The second a little less complex, Booze. Hard booze at that, white or brown. Whatever your preference.

For some reason in my experience, the guy that's drunk off beer just wants to kiss and cuddle. But the guy that drinks a fifth of Hennessy wants to fight. Maybe fuck later, but fight. Ironic? Maybe.

For the third and final ingredient of this Trinity Pie......... Trumpets PLEASE!........

Money People!!!

Like I really, felt like you should've seen this one coming! If you uncover enough layers, soon, you'll find the MONEY.

In this case surge hours during club closing time is where the money is. Which is 3am in Atlanta. People really start calling it quits around 2am, so the surge is always around the 2:45am mark. I guess that's some type of drunk persons reality that's it's just time to call it quits.

In any event with all the happenings in the Holy Trinity its always seems to be just the right recipe to make some $$money.

So, don't be alarmed. Now that you've been briefed, you should just begin to prepare when you see the ingredients coming together for "The Holy Trinity".

In your mind from now on, you'll just know it's time to pack some patients, and your wallet!

Ase'.

PRO DRIVER TIP 14

It's your car. It's your rules.
Don't think that spreading the rideshare love
makes you disloyal.
Drive independently and for all the rideshare
companies possible.
I stress to you; this is a business.

CHAPTER FIFTEEN

TWOTIMER

Pickup Location: Cumberland Mall Food Court.
Smyrna, Ga
Time: 6:22 PM

I love being my own boss. Start my day when I want. Saturday morning is my ME morning. Where I square off time for myself to take care of the important things that ground my sanity! I like to use this time to do things for myself that I actually want to do. Not the many things that I have to do.

This particular Saturday, I had an early brunch with my mom. A pamper Saturday. Just the girls hanging out and doing girl things. We got our nails/toes done after our brunch and ended the afternoon with a movie. Girls Trip, with Queen Latifah. We both love the Queen. She's so versatile as a celebrity, I really admire her. I've been on board since "All Hail the Queen" album debuted in 1989.

I was just a young tyke, but much like today I have always been a firm believer in the true status of my Queendom. I know who I AM. A queen acknowledges, embraces and gravitates towards like-minded planets, galaxy's and individuals that feel the same.

By the time I got home to change into some comfortable clothes and begin my evening of driving, it was about 5:30pm and traffic is pretty heavy. The downtown connector is at a standstill. So, I decided to hit some side streets to get back to the north where I intended on starting my Saturday night.

I went ahead and got off on the Mount Paran exit to cut thru Cobb traffic. I know I'll get a call when I get near Cumberland Mall on a Saturday.

Think strategically and most of the time you'll come out victorious. At least that's what's rang true for me. For the most part.

Approaching the mall, I get a request. Beep...Accept. The rider is at the food court entrance and his name is Terrance. This is an Uber Pool ride, so I made sure Terrance didn't have many guests.

When I pull up to the food court steps, I see my rider. He still has his phone in his hand. and he's standing with a female. They both get in, Terrance plus one.

They are cute and hugged up in the back seat immediately. I alert Terrance that we have one more stop around the corner before we began route to his destination. He doesn't seem to be pressed for time. He gives me the nod and the wink.

All good.

The next stop is the Aldi grocery store around the corner from the mall. It's about 3 min out due to all the traffic and stop signs. The riders name is Angela.

Terrance and his plus one is still making out in the back. Seems like a happy ride. I'm asking for the 5-star rating when I arrive at his destination. Gotta keep my rating prime.

Pulling up at the Aldi I see a sistah texting on her phone with a buggy and quite a few bags inside. I assume its Angela, but I call anyway to be certain. She answers the phone

Hey, Angela its Nico your Uber driver. I'm right in front of you silver car. I'll open the trunk and hop out to help with the groceries". "Thanks" Angela responds.

As Angela and I made some small talk by the trunk, she seemed tense or irritated by something. Her nose was sweating, and she kept blowing her hair out of her face. Like a person does when they are tired. I told her to get in the front with me. My back seat is pretty occupied.

Angela complied and sat up front. I got in too. We we're all set and the app dings for our first destination of the Uber Pool. Looks like Angela's stop, is up first. First stop is 7 minutes out. Last to pick up first to drop off. Sometimes its bees like dat.

We're in route now. Angela is on her phone and the couple in the back are still at it. The undertone of music is 90's R&B; TLC "Shoop" is playing at a medium tone in the background. Nice and mellow. I like it. Angela and I are singing and moving to the music.

I noticed looking in the rear view that Terrance and his plus one has come up for a little air with all the noise from the music and off-key singing belting from the front seats where Angela and I are sitting.

Terrance and his guest begin to talk amongst themselves in the back seat. Angela made a face in the front seat as soon as she heard his voice. As if she had heard something she wanted to hear again. You know that look, confusion and mystery all at the same time so to speak.

Angela reaches for the volume knob on my radio and turns the volume way down. She looks in the back seat and instantly became furious!

By this time, I am only about 2 minutes out from my first destination. Angela's crib. I don't like the tone or the octaves that are raised. This argument just began and there is already a fighting stance being given by Angela. She starts yelling 'OH REALLY!?' at the top of her lungs. She drops her phone on the floor in front of her and starts clapping her hands loud like she wishes it was Terrance's face.!

You know that clap.

Terrance, on the other hand can hardly say a word! His face is flustered, and his lip is hanging down. Like a motha fucka was 'cold busted'. An old slang term we used to use around the way when I was growing up. The short of things added up quickly to Terrance needing a lifeline or this was gonna have to be accepted as an L. Things weren't looking up for the young lad.

Angela was sure to not leave any information to chance. As women often do. She started spilling the beans!

She said, "I can't believe that I was shopping to make a great dinner for you since you lost your job yesterday'! "Wit cho broke ass!"

"Nigga you don't even have a place to stay! U Got 5 kids, that you don't take care of and I'm still making excuses for your triffin ass!! Everybody told me to leave your ass alone but NOOOO, I gotta follow my foolish heart!"

Angela is unleashing on this fool and Terrance has the same crazy look. Now his plus one isn't looking too confident either. By the look of things, I thought they both were about to whoop his ass.

Run Terrance RUN. Is all I'm thinking at the gate as we enter Angela's apartment complex.

Bro, ABORT! Now is good a time as any.

But obviously Terrance is a glutton for punishment, he stays seated. He begins to respond back to Angela's allegations with a mere apology. Like oops you got me! Drop the mic.

Shit now I'm looking crazy too. Like, Damn bro you just gonna let her talk to you like this? Un acceptable!!

Instead I say nothing and park in front of the building Angela told me. As soon as I park the doors swing open and Angela is in the back getting her groceries out. Terrance apologized to his plus one and got out of the car too. He grabs all the bags to help Angela and plead for his room and board.

Angela is heading into her building trailing quickly behind Terrance. She yells Nico and turns back around to head towards me. Angela's smiling as she leans over to me and slips me a tip and an apology for the eventful ride.

"Thanks Nico."

No problem I reply.

Plus one is still in the back seat, so I still have one more destination for this pool ride. I looked at the young lady and asked if the destination was correct or did she need to change it? She said no that's right. Stated how embarrassed she was and remained silent her entire 14 min ride home.

When I dropped her off, I realized something, wouldn't it have been ironic for the TLC song in the background to have been Creep instead of Shoop? Lmao, just a side note.

But for real, Terrance paid for it all. Ended up paying for both Uber pool rides dearly. Trying to be cheap in the first place. Then in the same ride ends up paying the major bucks for being dishonest. Costing him major points with his main chick and completely losing his side piece.

Now that's a battered man!

Lesson here: Take it from the kid. "There's no future in frontin playa."

PRO DRIVER TIP 15

Are you renting your vehicle to drive rideshare?
If you answered yes.
ABORT!
Do the math people. The numbers don't add up! Average payment is $250/wk. to drive. 1k a month?!
That's my hair note, my car note, my shoes note, my food note and my date note for the month!
I'm aware that life sometimes forces us to make difficult decisions…But try not start with deficit if you can help it!

CHAPTER SIXTEEN

NO TIP!? WHAT ABOUT THE DRIVER?

Pickup Location: Any Place, Uber Worldwide
Time: 24 HRS. A Day 365 Days A Year

When I started in this thing it was hot off the press. Brand new so to speak. I started in 2014 about two years after Uber launched. The rideshare service industry was just starting to buzz in the A. Becoming more and more popular by the day.

One day I saw this front-page article in the AJC, I just said what the fuck. Might as well make some bread in this process. Inside the advertisement, there was a bonus after like 250 rides or something. More and more headlines in the news about the rideshare industry changing the face of transportation.

I'm all about change. If things aren't changing, if there is no growth, your development is stagnant. Reinvent yourself. Reinvent your finances. As often and as necessary as possible. You'll find your true purpose and begin to write and rewrite the blueprint. I am a firm believer in this practice. I've learned so many incredible lessons from sitting at the feet of my elders. As many of the lessons were in unexpected places. Learn something valuable about life from an unexpected source.

That goes for businesses as well as individuals. So, Uber, here's a little help.

U can thank me later.

What's up with the tip option in the driver app? Isn't that the same shit you're getting sued for right now? Allegations of taking tips from the Uber Eats drivers. (By the way I never agreed to do that. I am not a food delivery driver. That's a completely different animal). Besides, where I'm from you don't wanna be a pizza delivery driver, anyway. That's like having a security position you DON'T get paid for at the same time.

That's too many fucking jobs!

Why would you have a driver rate button that is addressed after every single rider completes a ride? Yet there is NO TIP button at the completion of the rider's app?

Does that mean Uber doesn't think good behavior should be rewarded?

Maybe they think it's not Ubers responsibility to go to bat for the driver? To ask for the tip.

Could it be that Uber is too busy worrying about a cover for their own asses?

May it be wages etc. Or maybe it's the fact that Uber already charges an additional fee for the ride?? Uber is trying to make out like a bandit. Stealing all the safe ride fees for their own personal gain. Either way, the cats outta the bag.

Uber is already bleeding as a business with all the high salaries came cuts and layoffs recently.

Reported just yesterday Uber has decided to take an even closer look at their P&L. Afterwards, they decided to omit their $200,000 per year balloon budget.

Balloons? For real? 200k?

If I had the audacity as a business owner to include balloons on my P&L. Which is extremely bizarre. That speaks volume for itself, as well. Unless your business is called PARTYCITY.

Bad business practice, there's nothing else to be construed from these findings.

If Uber can somehow refocus and make the driver part of that focus that would show some true effort and initiative in the right direction.

The people.

The same people who keep your business model afloat. The same people that without them your business crumbles. You can't do it without US.

Even without the tip app. There are some decent folk left out there; that still think regardless of the app I'm still going to tip. Because in service; that's the appropriate thing to do.

Personally, in my tip experience has been many. All types of tippers. From that little old lady that tips some change or someone that gives you the proud dollar so to speak. All the way up to that $100 bill in the middle of the night.

By the way Benjamin either makes you want to go hard, or it makes you want to go home!

I've had that pleasurable felling three times in my rideshare career. Pretty awesome to feel like damn, I must be pretty good at this shit.

To conclude, Uber get with the program. There are good drivers out here who bring the 5-star service, every time. You should pay them.

So, Pay up!

Goodness knows Ubers reputation needs work. Each positive rideshare experience speaks volume for Uber as a unit.

Add tip option to each ride. Give up the cash, you didn't earn it1!

Play fair.

Your welcome!

PRO DRIVER TIP 16

Dear Driver,

Your appearance matters as well.
Your car should be clean, and you should be
clean too.
Remember:
Nobody has ever flattered a crowd with their
"Before" picture.

Thank you for reading my book!

The Uber Diaries: Atlanta Edition is the first book in a series of books from Taylor Made Publishing LLC.
If you are a rideshare driver and have had some memorable rides, you may be the next author in our series!
Even if you have thought about writing but just don't know how to start. Taylor Made can help!
Contact Taylor Made Publishing LLC
taylormadepublishingllc@gmail.com and/or log onto to
TaylorMadePublishingLLC//Facebook

I really appreciate all of your feedback.

Nico.

CPSIA information can be obtained
at www.ICGtesting.com
Printed in the USA
BVHW081406220919
559079BV00001B/7/P